Good
Character
Traits

Courage

Ashley Lee

Explore other books at:
WWW.ENGAGEBOOKS.COM

VANCOUVER, B.C.

ℓ WWW.ENGAGEBOOKS.COM

Courage: Good Character Traits
Lee, Ashley, 1995 –
Text © 2025 Engage Books
Design © 2025 Engage Books

Edited by: A.R. Roumanis
Design by: Mandy Christiansen

Text set in Myriad Pro Regular.
Chapter headings set in Anton.

FIRST EDITION / FIRST PRINTING

LIBRARY AND ARCHIVES CANADA CATALOGUING IN PUBLICATION

Title: Courage / Ashley Lee.
Names: Lee, Ashley, author.
Description: Series statement: Good Character Traits

ISBN 978-1-77878-722-5 (hardcover)
ISBN 978-1-77878-728-7 (softcover)

This project has been made possible in part by the Government of Canada.

Canada

Courage

Contents

What Is Courage?

Courage means doing what you think is right even though you are scared.

It means dealing
with things that are
hard even if you do
not have help.

Why Is Courage Important?

Courage helps people get over their fears. It helps them reach their **goals**.

Courage makes people strong and ready to try new things.

Key Word

Goals: things that people want that they work hard to get.

What Does Courage Look Like?

Courageous people stand up for what they believe in.

Key Word

Courageous: having courage.

They make good choices. They do not give up when things are hard.

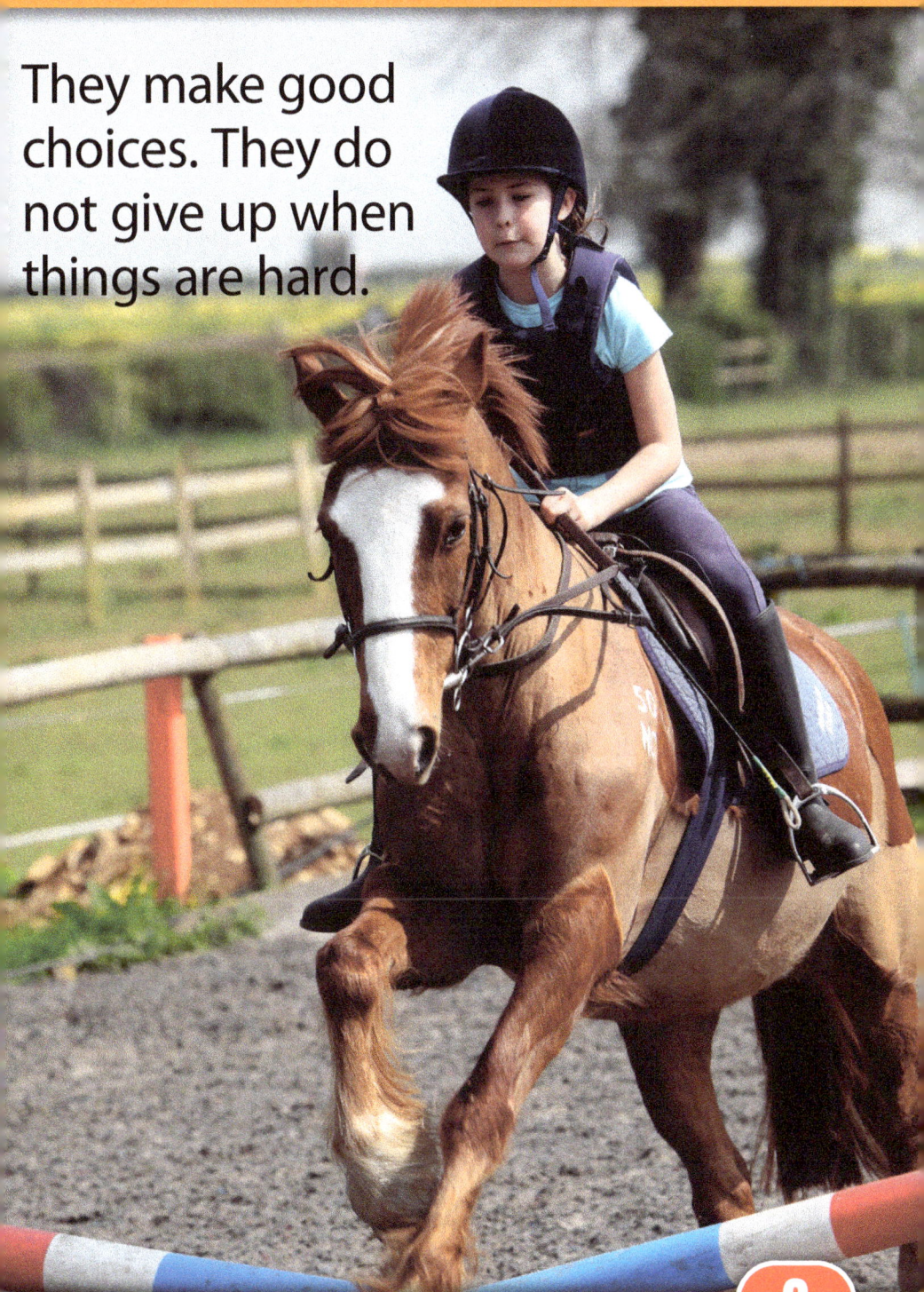

How Does Courage Affect You?

Having courage makes you feel good about yourself.

It can help you be more **independent**.

Key Word

Independent: able to do things on your own.

How Does Courage Affect Others?

Showing courage can make other people want to have courage too.

People believe they can face their own fears when they see other people doing it.

Does Everyone Have Courage?

Everyone can have courage. But not everyone is courageous all the time.

Everybody is afraid of something.

Some people have more courage than others.

Is It Bad if You Do Not Have Courage?

It is not bad if you do not have courage. Feeling scared is normal.

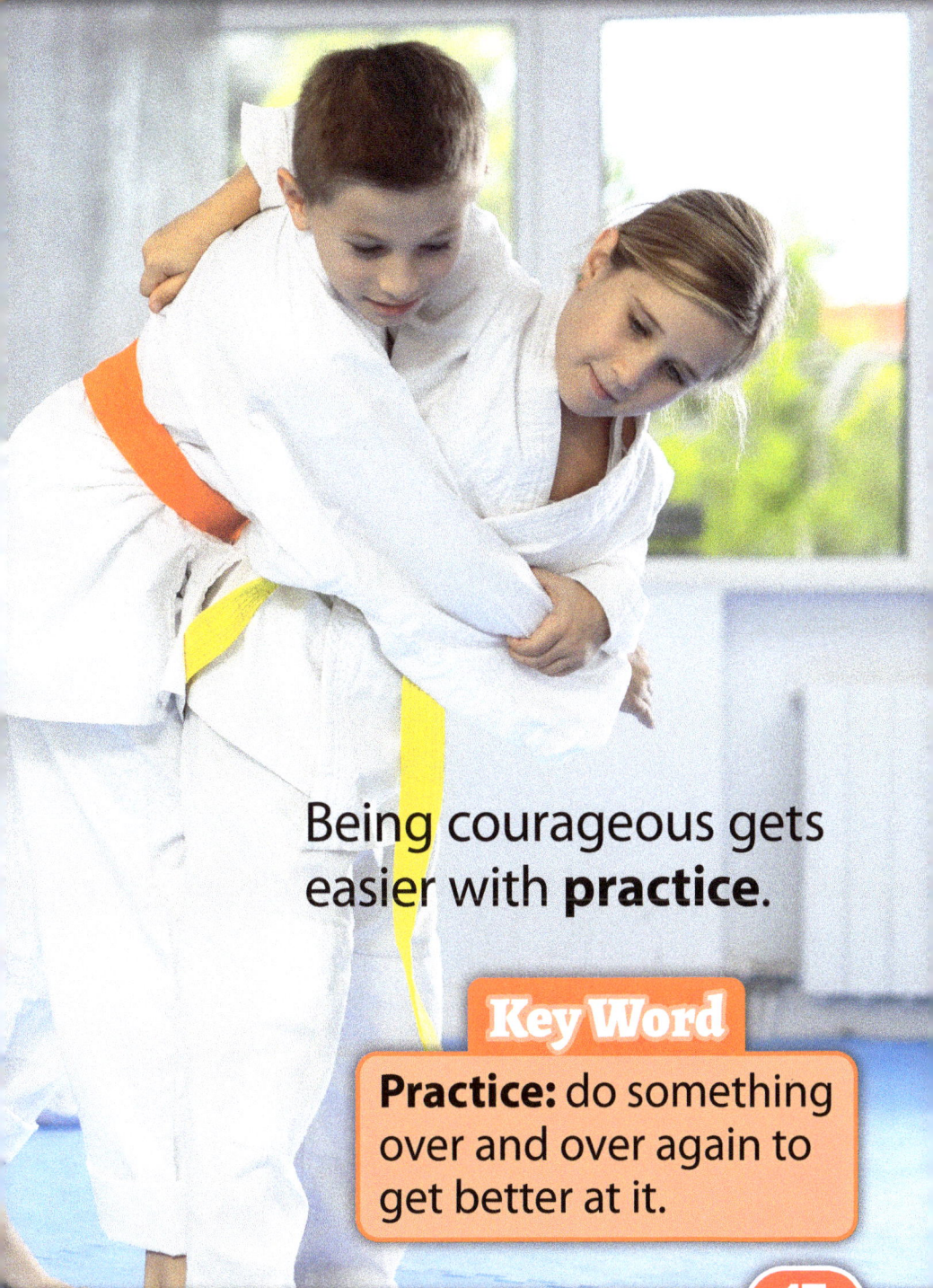

Being courageous gets easier with **practice**.

Key Word

Practice: do something over and over again to get better at it.

Does Courage Change Over Time?

People often become more courageous as they get older.

This is because people get more courageous each time they face something hard.

Is It Hard to Have Courage?

It can be hard to have courage when you are scared.

Many people want to run away when they are scared.

It can also be hard when people try to make you do something you do not want to do.

How Can You Learn to Have More Courage?

Think about your fears and ways you can **overcome** them.

Key Word

Overcome: to win against something.

Act courageous to help you feel courageous.

How Can You Help Others Have More Courage?

Stand with your friends when they face their fears.

Being courageous is easier when others help you.

Celebrate people when they face their fears.

Key Word

Celebrate: do something fun for a special event.

How to Feel Courage Every Day

1. Try something new every day.

2. Tell others your ideas.

3. Stand up for
your friends.

4. Say sorry when you
make a mistake.

Courage Around the World

People all over the world try new things so they can learn about Earth.

People would not have **explored** space or the oceans without courage.

Key Word

Explored: searched or looked into something.

Quiz

Test your knowledge of courage by answering the following questions. The questions are based on what you have read in this book. The answers are listed on the bottom of the next page.

2 Do courageous people give up when things are hard?

1 Does courage help people get over their fears?

3 Does having courage make you feel good about yourself?

5 Is it bad if you do not have courage?

4 Is everyone courageous all the time?

6 Can it be hard to have courage when you are scared?

Explore Other Level 1 Readers.

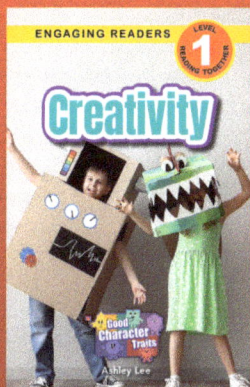

Creativity

Positivity

Resilience

Respect

Self-Control

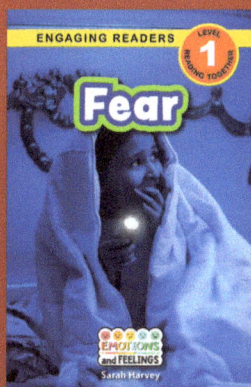

Fear

Happiness

Sadness

Surprise

Visit www.engagebooks.com/readers